WITHDRAWN

Compline
2556 Frances Street
Oakland, CA 94601
Compline.tumblr.com/
Cover Art: Harris Johnson
ISBN: 978-0-9835045-6-6

Withdrawn
Thom Donovan

Everything will be taken away...

‡

Or what I mean by this can't matter
The grave will just be a hole
My self some sense of self
Will be a hole when I am done singing

A place where I lost you of course
Where I stopped world forming
There would be a politics in this
If loss could be felt and not seen

It is easy not to sing
The face withdrawn from smoke
Different than a soundtrack
That never was for us

Expressing this limit that face
Makes signals in the air
Only that face understands
Because it can't stop remembering

The total catastrophe that was the line
Or the face wishing this
Wishes invisibly
In a language of these days

We became crossed-out
You burned your photographs
To remember home

~~A kind of body torn apart~~
~~A kind of body shared~~
~~A kind of body no one shares~~

Wishing the mind
To touch anything
But this combat

Combating, that is,
To touch you
And touching

Only dark, a room
Full of dark
All voices eyes

All I's be hushed
Sensed so stricken
As of in silence blowing

Whereupon the woman
You are the man
The skin sheds us

She singles herself out
Pointing out the lack of
Form in her self-apprehension

A failure to withdraw from
Them because every
Thing is in relation

What it would take
To name ourselves
Into unblind threat
To maintain this threat
And through it call
'Self' into being

Black light, black light
Of the light-skinned
Face cornered
In the room (any
Place whatsoever by
Your camera)

Any name, by the name
We would assume
How it would
Accuse an angle
And without alibi
Unworld

If they are not paid
To eat any fucking
Thing they want to eat
Whenever they want to

And not abide
By their illest purchases
On wanting to be
On wanting
To be in the world

The scar that could be made on their backs
Will be made on their backs
Because we can

The scar that is someone's power
To pay them and never
A living wage is a striking thing

Living in this discrepancy
The risk of losing you in me
Becomes something to sing

Nearly in the sea like water is in water,
Land within land, dreams with dreams

But then there are things we see with our desire
The deaths we are also with, apart inside us

Swell sometimes, speak to me a barometric
Of address and the consequences of not speaking

Of withdrawing from what we say, to another
Wilderness the dark will not pray for us

The dark will be a ground we recover in the night
Illegitimate, turning to those other bodies

Those others who are the only spirit, the only health
We will have known, going to them like conditions

To imbibe the harm that also involves us
Like forms for an approaching wreck.

‡

The Leak

Disaster's the national pastime
Shame's the natural course
Of hegemony sovereignty equals
Its weight in force

Disaster knows no limit
Limited only by the eyes
That see it not the decibels
Charged by their screaming

Rubble sees in retrospect
From the distance of their failed
Infrastructure from the distance
Of dispossession a kind of curse

Of progress what dispenses
With the ego society no force
Of nature accomplished this
Because we've gone global

And seeming
And a semblance
They flee
From us

The products leak
What one has been
Will be

Like a hole
In the transmissible
Air the sea
Is anarchy

Deregulating
Birds wings
Landing
Whole worlds

In imploding
Debt
Who gives
Their word?

Who are called upon to leak
All barriers of the same
And what we are and when
We are not reconciled

The way the ground rose up
Spills our guts makes us, um,
Come clean; spreads the
Shittiness around at least

Endless streams of stars
Crossed by song unweaved
Recall what won't be sung
Because no one is dreaming

It seems I can almost touch
The plume they cannot plug
Me up with currency and currents
Touch everything we'll never be

Copulas of cant
Evacuate what's left of place
Signify while real eyes watch
A wreck of belief

Not even time to mourn it seems
The loss of me as you
The event and the time this event
Takes place within without name

Because you were moving with it
Interrupted by the social
Interrupted by how language
Mediates the social

There is still a horizon here
A rose rim for the real.

‡

Mic Checks

"...the ear is the only orifice that doesn't close."
—from Sharon Hayes' *Parole*

Your silence blows the
Ears off my head

So that what I'm hearing
And what isn't seen
Structures the rupture

What's left-over
From speaking privately
In a public place

Some ways to imagine
Not being them,
Being crossed out
Or simply tongue-tied

If the tongue
Had eyes and they
Were here

If they
Looped like history,
Like the history of
A scream

Or steam from that
Whistle not yet blowing

The voices absent in this present
In their presence coheres a statelessness
Without subject

Sentiment is the tenuous
We screaming again,
Words one lip-synchs for their life

Discourse schools a public void
In private just because
You put a mic

On me doesn't mean my voice
Will carry

Or anyone is out there listening

We are archivable, which means
We can easily be forgotten

We are public, which means
We are double/multiple/substitutional

Through no lack of repression
Do the words finally appear

However private we are, however
Rich our interior life

[politics which pressures the inside out]
[politics will smoke us out]

[politics will drive us into the world]
[politics will drive us into the open]

Where any one may listen

To this resonance pattern
To these distances wherever you go
Voice a form of intimacy without control
Emotions before they formed and hardened
Into a public speech

Which summons us all these voices verbs
Recorded but not heard
Stricken from the record it would seem
Before sound could appear
Thinner than the thing-in-itself
The magnetism of all lost futures

In the breaks silence sticks
Wakes the dead from trace

The living from paradise
Semblance sleeps in our ears

Across eras cross-fading
Hatch private spaces in public

Tongue in my mouth in
Your mouth mic checks.

‡

The New Us

When bodies become the case
Will they still be a poem
Or form of art or prose because
Grief is a form of action

When bodies become the case
Of all we cannot be
No art can prove or disapprove
Movement made a maze

Of skin when bodies became
The case an image they still needed
That would extend space that might
Buy some time, save some face

For the dying whose bodies became
The case and were a law
Living inside the heart like
The law was always made

Blood becomes a site
No glove will heal or hold
Steeped in what was left to fill
Until hell evokes a reason

They put their hands on us
No glove will hold or touch
The law their bodies were
When there was no justice

So all the lenses of your
Camera almost crack
But don't outliving the fact
Of their blood's gaze, its resolve

That all our laws lacked
The question of this subject
What the body can do
Determines a line of police.

—AFTER ACT UP

The body is an archive
The breath a convolute
A collection sung for no one
But to remember it has danced

Compendiums when you point
With your eyes to what it did
And cannot do, this also being useful
The body fails but it survives

The body as an archivist
Kissing all relation, tells us what
We did, the failure of this doing
Called career, called smallest hope.

—for Jérôme Bel

The mountains around the city
Sounds they make blue
On the retina in the ear
Resound a commons what will have been
The time of year not weather
Not the names of these
Places no longer there
The people we took never given back
To a useless and unused air

There are plenitudes in what we do not
Possess, in which sound dispossesses
Our future property took like the real
Announcing exactly where we are
In relation to who or what externalities
Banalities like belief

So hack spirit, come hack this
Spirit enclosure up, talk to the man
Like he won't come back from empire
Like power can't do anything about this

So hack spirit, hack me up
Take my name or don't take it
Multiplicity see if I care

Division matters because we are born
That strived-for-never-in-fact-
Existing-ever-imminent-commons
In our swagger in fact matters.

—for The Kootenay School of Writing

Summons that we feeling
Certain things made
Gathering as a kind of making
An active question that storms our thinking
Called world, how we do
How we no longer called this 'us'
When a name was true
We lost our names
When loss was useful

Except capital
Except a certain
Knowhow the birds know
Their sense turning to sense
Their uneven development
Movements disaggregate
Subtracted from action
The air we make and the air
Which makes us
The *we stamp* and *we are stamped*
So complicity becomes the subject
So history isn't just a motor of mistakes

The new us starts from a dish
Not socialism, continues to grow
Sans system, an attention
To this consumption system, a local
Kissing of totality what will be value

And what's the use, in poking
Our heads out, food sovereignties
Produce this singularity

The new us, the new good life
Well being as muse and health
As wealth all we are saying's
The all new thing, new expression
Being shares this sense, of turning
Around a land, or land fills
Me up with emergence, political
Like a dish we cannot help
Gathering around, or con/tem/plating.

—AFTER F.E.A.S.T.

Let art lay fallow here
And artfulness since resistance

Fuels 'the system,' scratch that
Since resistance is part

Of an organum of control
A matrix of complicities

Stop the world simply let
It be useless, let be the silence

Of a different effort
Sing that it is elsewhere unframed

That conscience and com-
punction are a kind of form

Caring withdraws eclipsing
Art's acknowledged value,

The efficacies of its being for us,
Not an unspeaking thing.

—AFTER A PHRASE BY SLAVOJ ŽIŽEK, QUOTED BY J. MORGAN PUETT

‡

I am testing a series of propositions about friendship and community which may or may not last in time or produce the results I would have wanted or intended

I am testing them against the tried ephemera of political action and reflection on this action called theory even while it may be occurring

No dream encompasses this contradiction between what we dream and how we wake up and an effective mode of action within a particular set of forces or relations

Thus the feeling one is doing nothing while one is in fact doing everything

One must act very specifically while maintaining the possibility of everything.

‡

True Black (I)

"It's all black, I love us."
—Jay Z

1.

Death will come
For us it will call

Itself scarcity
The wind in the

Trees and meadows
Recall ruins re-

verse a process a
Social process if

We will be on time
And dust collects

What dust collects
On the things we

Built unsustainable
Like eros unifies

The ego it is a lan-
guage but I don't know

What it says, shit
Builds like sound

Concrete in my head
No longer dreamt

Nor will waking
Discover me a memory

Trace, a set of planes
Traversing blue

Ghosts of a geometry
Your horns blow.

2.

What worlds end
So we can create

Sustain caesura
A break of each

And each recall
The sea a rhythm

Of this place pul-
sing under what

We dream emer-
gent in the ones

We name sing-
ularities what we

Cannot possess
What genealogies of

Men won't colla-
borate with history

Since history
won't corroborate

The sense of ru-
ins revealing you

Dreaming us up
Not the other way

Around the sun
Clicks off and on

Soundlessly ab-
andoning to events

What we would
Call presence.

3.

These shiny
Stone-like cubes
Obsidian of what

They speak an
Alphabet cannot
Be said it is

Too much just
To feel them
To have to

Form words
Before pictures
Is a problem

Of history but
You know this
The glissando

In our politics
Of attention gliding
Cannot know

Us or call
Us back to
Kill whitey

So easily as
Antagonism art
Thrown into

History and
Not wanting
To be

Thrown into
An archive
Becomes responsible

For opacity
Assume this
Power not

Quite one
Making nothing
In particularity

It waits the thing
Itself to know
Ourselves.

—for Adam Pendleton

4.

"It's holy work and it's dangerous not to know that 'cause you could die like an animal down here."
—Abbey Lincoln, quoted in Fred Moten's *In the Break*

Like the heart was a line
Was a frame to break
A kind of intervention before
The score was made

Or everything could be written down
Totally administered worlds
Poetry becomes a score
It becomes a music that heard justly
Is never just heard

Performed but not played
To blow that supplementary horn

What we sing remains
Of that communication that is not their dreaming
Which is all a scream was worth.

‡

The Archivist

Because you wanted the world to hear
What you heard
Ears are all we are sometimes
A moment of music on them

The details not the mirage of *hearing*
That's what the archivist sees
Like we were sometimes just eyes
No longer I when we see
Stein said that
Because the world is mindful

Of identity you were taping it
All the time even the noise even the blanks
Before they organized our memories
What was even searchable
As memory

How any of it could impress us
This is where music comes in
Structuring the thing otherwise
All that time with the tape rolling
Just in case there was music

—in memoriam David Nolan

‡

For Robert

My friend when you go away
Into a medical emergency
An emergency of how living
Is practiced I miss you

I feel I am missing out
On my own life the consequences
Of which a building never
Materializing would make it true

Because the building is never
Built it remains a proposal
Or plan about how prosody
Lifts the body outside itself

How *ekstasis* cures
Your books remain to be written
Because the possible
Doesn't end with words.

‡

Park

I want to make a park with you
Make a campfire in the park
Like Mylar crinkles like light
Is durable the light we make

I want to make a fort where
Melody was and our voices were
Where our voices became a
Collective cry in the lost air
And yet uplifted and somehow
Spoken

Not in heaven, not into its hands
Not enclosed the voices we do
The fences we defend,
Bodies full of pain unmake
The world because they are not just
A language, never were they full
Of grace the toxins structuring us.

—for Kathy Westwater & Jennifer Scappettone

⸸

Like names falling through
Old levels sounds like
In the open of the public
Eye we are vulnerable
Scrutinized not just for the poems
Sounds they make on the inside

How they still how they don't
Make us whole but the whole
World flickers the time
They take to get outside
And sense not just this sense
Of the mind's survival.

—for Charles Bernstein & Sreshta Rit Premnath

‡

Spilled in the language's veins
A militant regard
When will words be
A tool for something other

Than exchange watching us fuck
Them up in the dance with
Forces again
The city shine with it

Little estates make a little
Shit out of me
You are everything
To me dear abstractions fleeting

View of the thing from the thing
In itself trees move with us
Our disappearance
We disappear the world therefore

Appears flashes with
Thoughts difference spreading
In these leaves
Bifurcating futures

Like elements *huckleberrying*,
Like language sometimes
Squats in us.

—for Stephen Collis

‡

Criss-cross this chorus
Not marshaling us
The state of the soul or
The soul of the state
Is a formal feeling

An emotional thing
Swerving into the doing
Standing reserves and
Potential across personnel

Body of living labor
Gives me a sign
We are not done with you yet
This is the place we were born
And this the place we became

Slaves in an air other
Than our own
The indentured sing
Of power in a new form

But are not themselves we
Are not ourselves
Beholden to a brand
Locking the flavor in like value

If an emotion possesses us
If a theory of value signs
Off into the void let us rule
For another decade

Let our nets cast us larger
Than our appetites appear
For control or the armies
That we lead

With their hands blown-off
No longer forced to rule
Who will resurrect
What we could not feel
The first time?

—for Rob Halpern

‡

The violence of this voice
Smoothed into place
Shared like reason becomes
Afraid and believes

From this cloud this hand
Of the police reaching down
Teaches us things suddenly
Like the animals once

Taught us to be headless
The mind utterly mindless
Made of flesh and blood
And covering the streets

Sites certain dissensus
It only knows seeing red
The mind bludgeoned
By a force without grace

Around the null set
Possibilities of planks
Intone our total abandon
Power ripples from

Pure means like white
Eschatology without end
Pierces the simple
Shapes of our art

Differences they make
Like machines on the skin
Harrows become operative
And run our mouths

A course of law could stand
No earth nor other
Orders of being
Crowned by its waste.

—for Michael Cross

‡

She's Lost Control Again

—after Mika Rottenberg's *Squeeze*

It's not clear whether
She's lost control again

Or if these ties the ropes
And pulleys are binding

One cherry leads to another
That's all we can know

Scented fetishes in the
Global village of the elect

Affect has made them abject
It has made a fool

Out of processes
A montage of the orifices

Coursing through power
Saying it dumb in the

Wind like a name
We all can't share

Fisting what's without
Fingering the constellation

Baser games of telephone
Tell the nails to grow

A tale of power
Told by the soul at work

If above or below
These powers the boxes
Kept moving
If this was a game
We were making the rules
Up as we went along
As though within our
Own bodies without control
She's lost control again
We're just beginning
To manage her limbs
Like assemblage we shit
We perspire autonomy
When they tell us to
Only there is no me
And there is no you
There is no beginning
In other words to this
Process this continuous
Product producing our
Exception

Like in a harrows we sweat
Like in a vacuum of political
Control called representation
Called media saturated

We wake to this machine
The women already wake spinning
Their hair as if from gold
A myth of morning

The animals who make them awake
And who assist with production
Form an assembly line
Within an otherwise post-Fordist refrain

One lays in the grass
Like a patient or an object
How these women they are husbandry
And husband and husbanded

I want to call this rhizome
The endless exploitation extending without roots
From a thousand holes where power leaks
Conspires and condescends on bare asses
The ass without a face, the dehumanized ass
The face upon which one couldn't reproduce
When all we could do was produce
The hours expand, click into place.

‡

This Is Not a Performance

Gives me the back
The backside this dance
Does the butt but does it
Suffice to be an object

In this dance motherfucker
Reduced to steps, reduced
To hips, a kind of scream-
like script I am hinting at

Like shade light passes through
Light, like there was no
Beyond but what is social
What is a social material

Leaving me what's left-
over from the armor
Love makes up the difference
Motherfucker my only friend

Nice up this substance
Come shadow come on
Open up a window
Pull this ladder up into skin

Songs the object and songs
The subject refused to sing
Ring thought balloons
Make the black still truer

No equal signs, no commons
In this index of who you is
In the present
The archive betrayed us

Blindfolds around entire bodies
Like a pair of eyes all over
Your body, a dance that was both
A fusion and a wreck

The eyes remain the windows
Of the soul, but who looks in and
Who looks out's a question
Posed by your body.

—for Adrian Piper

‡

Blood Moon

Sometimes I feel
Like a fatherless daughter
A motherless father-
land under this sky
Overlooking blood

Tribe adrift with a
Flood of it, the
Inconsolable, unexplainable
Wreck of moral
Ressentiment, which

Like eyes replaced,
Like the heart re-
placed for politics,
For history, places
Blood came from

What you wouldn't
Bless then bless now
Isis, repair the
Labyrinth of those
Calls to be violent

Call forth women
To conquer their

Sons-filial-cells
To wreck identity
Replace it with

A new Indian-
Angel-step-moving-
me-up-to-the-sun,
Something older than
Blood—like a blood moon.

—after Etel Adnan

‡

Back Figure

Rückenfigur in reverse
Her hearse reviews
Give me the back
Spoken like a true muse
In starving time
Speaks to power
What names our name
Withdrew

Through embroidery
An effort to send
These names renewed
Into time say my name
Motherfucker be mine
Lapse from relic to
Wanting you
Earth is our studio

So you want to be said
Into history so you want
That gaze to be for you
All turned around
Capsized from the cross
All revolving things that
Devolve to an act of anthem
Like seeing you wasn't

Simply enough
Like hearing you blew
My ears off

I, you, and we,
We have become dis-
enfranchised equals this
Desire to see your actual-
statuary-backside
Of the face you are naming
Power with
Speaking truth to sunset
By seeking out shadows
Folds of your robe
If with a backward look
Took from that flatbed.

—AFTER RIGO 23

‡

Area

—after Renee Gladman

That little limit
Of the distance
Between ourselves

And the world,
Ourselves and event
Witnessing the haptic

Sense of the hand
Touching you,
The nipple tugged

And toggled
Beside one's self

That's what living's called
Unworked by everyday dreaming

Busses loop this place
We would be, this city

That might identify the body
If it were here

Or the crowd would not disperse

If we were anywhere
In this present and
Not dying from death

Which is different than
Actually having lived,
But not so different from
Writing—

A form of living with
Death inside a present
The words one writes
Withdraw us from

Like a camera
Swoops in it
Swoons and we
Are not unlike
It gliding in
A sense of one's
Own appearance
Among others

Where we meet
Where the body
Touches other
Bodies,

Like a world was
Ending

Come to your senses
Come up from air, for air
From all this mumbo jumbo

The distribution of the senses
We are living in a grammar
Of commons, the most beautiful

Myth while actually not being
In common most of the time
The body breaks-up space

Does not grasp it, reassembles
The surround called sunshine
Already lapsed to an idea

Of me or you heat involves
The light from this incident
The forethought of our lives

In this event, not on the inside
Are you beautiful to me
For all time, but being

Inside-out and twisted
Like a territory we experience
In real time while observing

What we are when we are
Not writing, social substance like
A tracking shot makes ‘me’ area

And moment and movement
—a type of twice dying one
Experiences before death took place.

‡

After Paul Chan's *Sade for Sade's Sake*

Body parts without bodies
Parts without parts

Anti-gravity pulls apart
The blue windows bits

Bytes silhouettes provide
Place increasingly crowded

Flicker with bodies ace-
phalics on their knees

Bleeding cubes float
At the beginning am I

At the beginning use
Of wall as cage as

Screen saver like the
Flicker like of a sudden

Shudder iconoclast Matisse
Color bars end piece

Activate constructivisms
Malevich black squares

Fall like the sky dangles
Appears institutional

Why Sade now why
Not Marx why not

Machiavelli or Spinoza
But for torture because

We are in a time
Of cruel affect and

Virtual commandment
Pornos squares

Are flat but create
Foregrounds contexts

The figures seen sil-
houetted like a Walker

Cliché (i.e., cut-out) they
Are gestural too these

Quivers shakes diddles
There is reference to Stein

Who overcame beginning
Again and again the

Porno of all narrative
Poetry will there be

An end to this again
And again goth animation

One commands with
Penis erect another

Trembles holding a
Square over their head

This giant negativity
Of what can't be seen

Partial objects (shit)
Fetish objects reliquary

Remains rubble debris
Something trapped inside

Anamorphosis slight
Blur every one's penis

Suprematist episodic new
Slaveries why would I

Destroy you once when I
Could destroy you ten

Thousand times (fascist
Aristocrats in

Pasolini's *Salo*) crawling
Holding lifting fucking

The limits of being
Human act bestially

Crawling on their knees
They make decisions

With their dicks carry
One another on others'

Backs there is also a
Spirit of Sade in labor

There is also a spirit
Of Sade in poetry.

‡

An Archive of Eyes

So close
We formed did
Drugs form us

An archive of eyes
To hear with you
The better

No one here but
Butterflies drawn
By some body

Flutter like the
Collective function
Of a madeleine

Mineral owls
Of Minerva
And material

Conditions sparkle
Like blind feeling fly-
By-night reports

Information every
Which way ablaze
With organs without

Bodies so ecstasy
Folds what the
Multitude do.

—AFTER FRED TOMASELLI

‡

All I wanted was to be in a band

—after a phrase from Fred Moten,
for Dana & Brandon

I just want to be in a band, man
And play anything ourselves out of here
Hear these tones like water stutters water
Like sunk ships suture the social or social
History was what we were immersed in
I hear your voice on the other side of disaster
What plays its way out of disaster
Just like it wanted to be, just like it wanted
To be in a band, convince us we are living
In a different future-past because the tones
The political economy of noise with its puncture
Of the present might wake/make a plinth
Through this struggle to be all-too-human
Come back from these feeling tones—
Assemblage, stutter, DJ function

The DJ functions like love
To spread these petals differently
To see we don't sing too sweetly
The stench of common sense
Wasted on your lips
Kissing me into which future
Like an ark of horns I
Haven't heard
Because I can't, I cant
With ears blown off
With an archive like
The tides are rising too
Into song and all those islands they will
Only seem to rise to it, drowned
These waves like a wall of sound
This is the remix of a disaster hymn
I made when no one could hum immune
Or even probably hear me

Could hear immune or America disappear
Into these people it disappeared
The atmosphere it sold the waste
It pretended was not for sale (displaced)
The waste it sold like gold,
The air it gave away

But I want to be in a band, still
Some unresolved, unforeclosed sociality
(That singing is) (That being in a band is)
Going down like Rimbaud, say
To announce an end to which pronouns
To announce the organs unformed by work
That begin in our play—
To prove that these hands are made and unmade
By the music any one makes
Who is not just 'me' singing
Through the violence of that voice
Or a name we impose
On something when we feel
It is special, particular—like a band
Needs a name, like one feels they need to
Distribute this feeling for being in a band
Protean form of revolt, like a public
Not quite public yet, in an assembly of notes—
Like a 'people' forms a public—these notes

I want to be in a band, man
Like Rimbaud wanted to be in a band
Or more likely wanted to be like all this stuff
The barricades were filled up with
During the Paris Commune, or so I imagine
After Kristin Ross's *The Emergence of Social Space*
Which my friend Dana turned me onto,
All that we are the lived duration of our sociality is like
Those barricades made in such a way
That all of these meanings—the meaning of
Our work and life—seem temporary, mutable and
Arbitrary, yet full.
I want to be in a band
I want to be full like those barricades are full
I want my life to have meaning—or measure?—
Like those barricades have meaning and measure
The whole world thinking about how it is being made
That would be a politics to strive to create.
The whole world represented by its being made, through its
Being made.
Gives up art to be a worker.
Gives up art to be an art worker.
Gives up politics for life.
Because life becomes politics.
I want to be in band, not just a group, definitely not just
Any public.
Because, as Fred says, there has never been a public
That wasn't denied to most of us, most people.

The public is what has been historically defined
By its exclusion of certain people and not others.
What would be a public
That didn't exclude us and others?
A band then? A really big band?

Is this the barely
Chiaroscuro of our moon-
like privacy breaking like
Our hearts privately
Into beams?

I want to be in a band,
A poetry band, this is for you
This wreckage Bruce and
Melissa, unlikely pair
Of you tonight

Anarchy of your
Alternative gathering spaces,
Aggressive affect and calm
The person starts again
From pure sound

Materiality of sound,
We are shock effects,
Hypnosis heard through
Orange command, holes we were
Sucked through

On our way to being,
Into another future, I want
To get this armor off
But rhetoric sticks
To substance

Like a permanent
War of subjects, where it wasn't
Clear who or what was subject,
Just that sense ignited
Some sense of us

Sound blows the armor off
And love remains from fire
Or rather phonemics
Like they were making space up
As they went along phonemics
The place where the voice
Is playing me a prosody of disaster
The regret in this light
Too bright like bad faith
Discovers command –
Expropriated camp and blues,
A reappropriation you can feel, pours
This discovery over horns
And chicken scratch skronk
Of a voice circa 1979
Birthplace of no wave
Apotheosis of punk

Blows the armor off
Our dance, conversation—
So show me whose blogging
Nowadays? What this is for, the subject
Losing control again—call this
Communal noise what won't be shared
Names the grave already a trace
Where you put it the sound of space-
Time occluded, where you put it
Our hearts beat diachronous like breaks
Over beats, wild styling this Lefebvrian city
Paris 1968, Paris 1871, Egypt 2011
And Vancouver forever, Cincinnati,
Friends of poetry

Hoping to avoid 'my' voice
Traveling any further than social space
Where the ink may dry—ex-
propriation of failure, here is the
Proper way to deal with property
Art thinking presents a whole
New range of problems
Like, hello, the product was autonomous,
Or the voice—only in a new way
There is territory—capital we still
Ain't delivered from—like
Parodies of Facebook only excel
In obsolescence timed to capital
So this movement started,
Poetry calls voices to battle,
To capital again

But I wanted to be in a band, really
And this being in a band (micro politics)
Free of coercion, modeling a world
Free of coercion, would be an exercise
In freedom—the assertion of language as
Freedom, maintained in the world's total
Construction (still a soundtrack is wanting)
And this would be, the dialogism emergent
In the sampling of the DJ function (love spreads)
Parallel universes to this one (failed) commons
This poverty of how the commons was imagined
Triaxial (Braxton) would sound us to a new mode
Play us out of the fucking little games of power
(that have played us) – unthinkable corners
Of our sociality and affect and work
Kids waiting for it on almost any corner or cornfield
Know it absolutely ordinary, absolutely common
Evental only after the fact (like any uprising in social fact)

All I wanted is to be in a band, man, I guess
That makes me an expressionist, I guess that makes
Me an anti-specialist, to want to trade instruments
With you non-instrumentally, mid-show
Like a K Records band or maybe Factory
Because they didn't know how to play them yet
We are off into some other way of being played
Some other commons in your hands and breath
Into the incalculable music plays irreducible
To number, how many we would number, what new
Powers playing our way out of power—if one
Were only in a band, I could talk to you, and idleness
Could set in between sets, riffs. Being in a band
Would be the only mode of work—goddamn plentiful.

‡

Commons

What remains if a commons isn't common? A gust runs through us, an organ on the outskirts or outside this having. A specific body the real estate inside us. Sometimes the air is disguised as being shared. We have given up what has forced us to give up on history. Someone says "you are good" when what they really mean is you are easily fucked over. Docility, like a syndrome, the students respond "my education that's what disaster surpasses me." My culture, what I have known, gives new meaning to entropy. The Dan Graham-like photo spread of crystalline houses. Split-entry like a place where the past breaks with the present and 'we' becomes compossible. There is no commons, no passage yet within this interior. Except where I made the first cut the ear began its work. Of obligation, patient like the obligation to be sung into silence, the wishes of aporia. When aporia is the only passage, no return, no name across this law, no crossing out. Or erasing the face is enough, or giving back, to bring those bodies back. They want/we want their/our cut of the pie. But only get this cut. Parts of the part in blind sunlight. Shade pulled until there was no world. When what I mean is: don't get used to the night.

Almost soiled my self—is this calculable?—the retreat as ever into being, always being. I can hear their digging like Renfield in Coppola's *Dracula* can hear all the insects and animal life underground. Fills me with a dread, telepathy of a thousand cranes developing, making vectors through my heart, my breath, my life, my love. Having harnessed the effort of a billion brutes where the commons is in actuality and what hasn't been imagined yet? Compossible like gestures, gene pools, muscle memory. Compossible like an affect transmissible in collective expression. The faces reflecting me before speech became lucrative, codified as perceptible song on some retroactive-impossible barricade. There are gestures we are making unawares (true force of multitude?) and rhythms other than having (been) worked. Rimbaud imagined work as the principal source of infirmity, immiseration, anti-sociality. All the things the species has done in spite of this. All the nobility—that specific bodies persist in their dance. Inventing worlds because 'I' is what remains from their invention. Because, incalculable, bodies persist specific to their dysfunction. What ruptures us, a fulfillment of *communitas*.

The legal anomaly of smog passing for unpotentialized fog. Is our actual dream in common. Is our nightmare systems move too quickly. The ocean pumps sound the world grinds to zero sums. Not because there is no consciousness, but because there is. The passage of clouds too quickly in our despair. First they sold-off our hands (remains), now it's time for our lungs, our skin. But I don't want to be a fucking last man. Fear of *amor fati* when we feel fucked in a global sense. What remains from your cynicism, sloughed-off. Bad affects abound across territories no one has the guts to legislate to regulate to legislate to regulate to legislate so we are all crowned fools. And if the whole world became a grave? And if your universalism led to a little island with perfect waves, a preordained sunset, a pile of cash—would we call this Robinsade or Robincide? Climbing over whose backs to the good life. No one even wants to save the moon. If not for the view from their little windows, which open while a million others close.

If there were some rainbow at the end of a truncheon. Coerce the crowd and call it art. Call it organization, set the museum adrift. A horse shits on the shiny floor. The voice of the police forms into a voice again. Visual quotations of that commons we've never been. If there were some rainbow in those words "crowd control." The voice of the father like a reign machine. In the 30s in the 60s in the 90s. Before we could represent as art the things that were being done to us/that we participated in/that we were doing. Left over from some rainbow, the blood of some truncheon, some whip.

‡

No one comes back
But every one comes

Love cut-up again
Like a fantasy we project

In these states the asshole
The mouth we shared

Lips know their way only
Not where they're going

The cunt like a fantasy
No thing returns as it was

All that was otherwise
Before our organs were.

—for Dodie Bellamy

‡

Rights of Participation

To let it out so that [______]
Can't use, blank that
Won't produce, that for now
Won't be a subject

Negates their using our
Emotions up in a public way,
Blocked by virgin forests
Participation reigns

Blocked by reified relation
Blocked by these tissues
The way this tear in the eye
Becomes commodity

An intellectual thing blocked
By the things we would share
So that [______] can't use
So we communicate today

What images won't remain
And names negated
By creative potential
Blocked by consuming the social

All that doesn't remain
Will be let out,
The tear in your eye when it
Won't become.

—after Not An Alternative

If this is called inclusion
Count me out

Love absorbs an order of the cops

Patrolling their reward
In paradise purportedly

Where a billion affects have failed
There is a feeling

Of freshness for you in me

Absorbed like a dream of losing you
Or being left behind

In the messaging of our waking dream
Affection absorbs a structure

Invisibly touched, patrolling its reward

If hell is friendship where a billion
"likes" have failed

What failed regard won't make us lose?

Coerced purposively in a perceived
Paradise to the point that I could feel

Anything, this body, I could feel,
Me in you

Absorbed like a dream of losing you
Lost in a messaging I am senseless to

The sun, like a blind spot in reflexivity
If this is exclusion count me in

Call me your remnant patrolling
Its little reward

Redemption of the world called us
With the words struck through.

‡

The beginning of worlds the diamond is
The facet is saved by space
Made coherent by all it isn't, messianic, an epic

Paper bag over the face
Of the whole world, world-covering
This is the covering of

The world not merely its end
What you affirm by saying it isn't
Shines radiantly like rest

Or silence when the world recedes
It resembles an ear
When we were not hearing, just listening

This was the soundtrack
To my soul
I say these things because I want to get over

My voice, do the
Voices you do
Waiting for the tape

To cut-off, the lip synch to appear
The body wholly voice
The angle of incidence it comprises

A fire so many have died for
Prismatically a universal bling
Compressed to this singular dedication

The products of culture
Form no ground
To base this love on

Yet they are all we have
Love of what is missed
In the absence of what we never had

Or could possess, this song
We just made up—here it is
The applause sign blinking soundlessly

Before the studio
Audience of our souls
The kind of participation that affect is

Crying tears on the inside
Diamond-shaped
Before they ever shone.

—AFTER DANA WARD'S "MY DIAMOND"

‡

True Black (II)

—for Glenn Ligon, Sanford Biggers, & Tyrone Williams

I see you in silkscreen stages
The *wrong nigga to fuck with*
Getting beaten for what is real
Social practice and what it belies

Immanent like paint writ over again
Or Walter Benjamin comparing his theology to a blotter soaked with ink
Or a text all these pictures might be worth
Meted into false equivalence

Some bodies aren't the same as others obviously
You took the black light literal that was your invention
To shine in this inversion of America like a blotter soaked with ink
Repeated until we are whole or blind with presence

Immanent like no description passes for witness
Repeated until we are one with violence
Until God is the nation no negation of negation
Or *via negativa* will do what we do

Just the sublime despair of cultural production
Messing with you in a white cube
Another name for this tomb
Repeated until we are resurrected or struck through

Until living labor can really live or art is allowed to die
Your own blotter shines like sunlight out of sequence
Playback of what was never felt the first time
Summoning the viewer

Cheshire Cat smile
Joker's smile
When you disappear
Every gleaming tooth is
Fugitive
Every light bulb flashing your word
Every word
We'll ever say
Or write down being the same
Like a language for our disappearance
Reappears again
Queen presiding
Some other powers that be
Chop our
Motherfucking heads off
Climb up a tree
And smile your head off
Until surveillance is
Just a dream
And this mask becomes the costume it is
Climbing trees that will never be
Just trees
Inverting Brecht's admonishment
Smiling our asses off
This is of course in reference to lynching
Not symbolism
Not the tree of life
Just signifying

All the masks we put on and
What else?
What the smile won't
Trade
Make its property
It overdoes
Overcomes
Lips shine a way
Through night
Flashing lights fucking with our heads

Life is repetition
(Gym, tan, and laundry)
Riding like a House beat
Over the heart, membrane of
That romantic organ,
Snooki plays dumb at another
Stupid job in another
City any shore
Of the multitude where people
Fuck, where people fuck
And cry their eyes out
The passions are in excess
To anything we mean
To discover there late
Late late in this twilight
Called credit, called brand name
Called ban, little houses
They live in and excursions
That everyone can believe,
Life is real but not recordable
This is what it means for it
To escape us

Trees rush by like equal signs
Blur a Detroit, a Cincinnati of the mind
No need to allegorize when bodies beat the fuck up
Do all the talking
Freeze frame on a stack of money
Worth more now as art
So a drive-by are we?
Chain gangs formed from broken signifying chains
Dip-dip-die (but mostly die)
Until we are socialized
Or drown, other voices run our mouths
Follow the money
Incorporate everything
Supposed to be a people
Follow it down
Into a nation language, uneducable
I heard symbols saying things I could not
The dozens do sublime
Damage to refrain
No equal signs form an action here
Snow sweeps down then there is no more music
Striving for protection in a music
Of contestation
Becoming uneducable the mouth
Opened-wide, keyed to black rage
Like in *Candyman*, all those empty
Mirrors we can't wake up from
Don't know how we got here

Music why be alive
When for all eternity it's like he says
Rhyming will right our names
Bees fill the mouth with muthology
Phonocentric, buzzing before the image captures
Spirit and image
Of our separable selves returning
Noise decorates what context debuts
Refusals in projects housing
Music though this is not music
Keyed to white rage blowing-up
The spot we howl
A national unconscious
No equal signs 'tis of thees
Demolish refrains, appropriate and detain
Why be alive when all we do is dream/scream
Educate the mouth to love noise.

‡

Since Zuccotti

What the opposite
Of *habeas corpus*
Is dissolves with
Your hair on my face,
Your legs around
Me without demands
Agreed upon in advance

The problem is to
Make us an us
Without making us
An us, to keep
These pronouns
At arm's length,
Touching proper names
Like the singular becomes
Multiple

No people was ever
Separable, no dialogue
From what it intends,
The abuse of the abused
Must end, the undead
Move through these
Lines thinking the
Necropolis, thinking
The polis after it was

Not one of them
In the place they belong,
Like I or you wasn't
The remnant,
Sublime kernel of
Wanting to be a citizen

Here is a list of all the things
I did while revolution was fomenting
Or while we watched something
Happen on the sidelines
In Facebook:
Now's your chance!

Peopleless I didn't want
Of anything but freedom ripped

From life after austerity policed
Full employment Whitman

Never predicted this synthesis
Yet for a different kind

Of totality do we spray
The will within populations

Saying what won't be defended
Because natural rights aren't given

We risk losing the whole periphery
To be in this sea writing.

Hedges grow like deficits
Inflation does more work breed
What you see but do not know
What you are doing and know too well
Concrete like money, like the air is heard

Abstract like a surface and
A surface just beneath
The visor called finance
Visualize a difference
These markets make on the skin
Visualize the end of the world
Then stop it since these
Distributions form a name

I know these waves don't shelter me
No shelter was their song
They gave to me American
A kind of islander in a divine

Wind, its exceptional breath
When we take our last whole worlds collapse
Whole markets collapse proletarianizing

What we touch, even ourselves,
No longer immune to this gift

Shadow speaks with me
Is this the scarcity
We were dreaming of
The people we were
Inside the people
Light outside
In the trees no repeat
Performance is this singing
Like praise they rise
Up singing
Speaking not knowing
Where body ends pre-dawn
In the park somnolence
Gives us reason.

So we were the police a sign of dissensus
Decry force little anthems we tell ourselves
Little voices we were bright curve
Of the object we were when we learned

To frame no one labor caved for no one
Because equality rests on process no politics
Without poetics says you Plato was wrong
About a lot of things get over your philosophy

This is an interruption of ethics
For politics or simply the way things should work
When we don't how we get down like that
In the early streets in the swarming streets

Abandoned by the national discourse
Sunset of that discourse this is dawn
At least police if you won't come to our side
Spray your own eyes out so you might see.

‡

People are Making Shitloads

People are making shitloads
This disconnect
The advantage of the absorption
Making shitloads
To close the system
To close the system not
To open, disclose
Shitloads, people are making
Is a service
Is a service when this not being
It is clearly an invitation
This sense of loss
To close the system
Is towards the beginning of ideas
People making shitloads
Devastate quality
As a response to absorption
Is a service
This disconnect
Is a service
This sense of loss less as ephemeral
Than a failure
To close the system
The people make
Making shitloads
To open, to disclose

But it is not 2008
That constitutes a lag
In advance of witnessing
The system collapse
Of witnessing
The system from within
This sense of loss
People are making unamplified
Inside the people
Less as an ephemera than
A need to surround buildings
Produces the world one
Is hearing beyond control

Give me a mic check and
I'll give you the world
People being made the
People being made
While the mic's not on
Are you hearing the sound
Of the world
Surrounding buildings
Whose murmurs were control

Up in this city finally plausible
Beyond control
Give us the world
And we won't divide it

Like the pie divides what
Do you hear
People making shitloads
Now they are heard
Pie charts now they are
Ripples in the middle of
The people
Intoning the air inside me

So what we simulate
Is indivisible
From the sounds we make
Like Stein
Says explanation people making
Shitloads
What do you hear
The people being made
While we hear
Where a process begins
Beyond control
A people swells
Inside the ear.

—after phrases by Ben Kinmont,
composed for the "People's Microphone" at Zuccotti Park

‡

Dumps

There are dumps
And then there are dumps
Violent like sunlight
Hides in methane
Like a heathen/Eden of capital
Literally farting up a storm
Of paradise, a kind of last frontier
Of our thingness
Last men do it all night long
Until we all become subject

Methane, last bastion
Of property relations
Called pollution erstwhile
Profitability is our fatal
Enclosure threats of extinction
Literally fart carbon
Cash rules nothing moves
But the money
Out of the island Staten
Home of the Wu Tang Clan
And retired police of course
They closed the schools around
The dump for capital

For methane, the most absurd
Thing was these dumps were made
At all, now a profitable farting
Shitting us our common fiction
Of ecology & capital
Coexist these are the levels
We are dealing with
The unthinkability of waste
While endgames take place.

‡

The ingestion of one substance
We are making
That we are making
The world up as we are also
Movement and we are built
To move in waste our ways otherwise
Than being what you have to say
When breath becomes bread
And there seems no other way
But in this dance other forces sway us
We are persuaded like the world twists
The way it depends on bread
Everyday to sustain
The simplest things
It is the simplest things that are
Easiest to forget
If we ever remembered them at all
I am using the line as a continuous breath
Not a metaphor for things seen
Like we can breathe our way out of this immiseration
Pivot and pirouette our way out of debt
Out of the pollution of everything
To assert the fourth dimension
Betrays our sympathy
And not merely our power over, as Pound claimed,
The animal
To leaven this sense of awe again
The power of things over words, that would

Be bread
Making the world up as we move
These built lines of song
These step-like tones
When time and justice should be one.

—for Chase Granoff

‡

Debt (I)

The *crays*'mas lights
All come greet me

Cape Cod all come what
Beacons X-mas taps

Thee out when
Light is about returning

Not just birthing
"It is a cold world"

The cab driver says
While I tip him, "have

A good life if
I don't see you again"

His repartee is
Good natured

But rehearsed, nights
On Cape Cod in the winter

Some places are pitch-
Black the highway

Like the sea undulates
They are foreclosing,

He tells me, on all the
Houses the greedy

Got greedier
The wicked wickeder

This year you can't
Convince me after 40 years

Of this shit that it can't
Get worse but I swear

I love the Cape
Without people

David Graeber's *Debt*
Is on the kitchen table

Of my parents' house
I haven't read it

Yet it has the seduction
Already of something

One should read to feel
They are part of their

Generation, this poem
Is for all my friends

December 22nd,
2011 I don't want

Any of you to die,
I want us to live

The best we can,
Let the (living) dead

Consume themselves
I believe

In interruptions,
Not endings.

‡

Where it proceeds to the rupture

Is experimental where it proceeds to the rupture

of the cultural model, lights were struck
and bitter coffee served, interrupted

every half hour for feedback how to share
an experience that produced

such profound changes in one's self?
Art making, an ambiguous expression

of personal and collective desires
A glance or tear, a media intervention,

the modulation of affect in the face of that threat

Seattle happened here then was foreclosed
What's the use of aesthetics if you don't have eyes to see?

They drank the bitter coffee, interrupted the projections to bear witness
The affective modulations that won't be represented

without eyes to see them with

Who drank out of empathy the affective modulation
Of our ambiguous desires, neither personal nor collective,

Yet political all of them before any of this was subjective
Or in a white cube

Because these tears turn to [_______] no one will see

Things you heard, you are trying to remember them hard
No one will know the things you heard

When what we remain are powers.

Post-expectant, the heart at work,
what should we name its book, lovingly?

Messianic aspect of a place from which to begin,
actual birds drenched, withdrawn from post-expectant

springtimes somewhere else there are worlds,
somewhere other than [_______]

Which like William James' polyhedral turns
thousands of miles above our infancy, blue and rarefied

Subtle like a conversation, the world does not
actually begin, it begins and ends suspended

by friendship, by enmity announcing the proximity
of end times, where it proceeds to the rupture of the cultural model.

—AFTER SOME PHRASES FROM BRIAN HOLMES

‡

After *Dark Matter*

You put the dark back in dark matter

Sweet corporate window that closes when we don't participate,
Take up the pixels code of a different world

Miniatures make their mark and so do stencils
Mimesis of a digital commons just out of view

Like the way we feel controlled even when we make
Something new, express ourselves into freedom's semblance.

Chris Marker says in *Sans Soleil,* "If they don't see happiness, at least they will see the black"

Which I take to mean that blindness becomes a condition of possibility
For seeing historically,

Like moles burrow in unredeemed soil, that "black leader"
Seeks a prophylactic to the appropriating powers
Which have led to our subterranean despair
At the failure of images to produce totality

Now we quote thought balloons in caves
Now insight becomes its antithesis unawares

Dreaming when we cannot scc
Waking from the archive again.

—for Gregory Sholette

‡

What We Are Doing

"The progress of our naiveté," Rachel calls it

Socrates says that one knows just enough to know that they are being naïve

How we reveal to the public what is not known to it because it is not known to us

The artists occluded like day laborers their shacks on the outskirts of luxury hotels where a tarp gleams white in the sunlight

What does the world cover to be the world?

Miles of fertilized food only some will get to eat

Making this knowledge public makes for broken instruments

Everyone must eat but only scarcity is consumed in the control society

Levels of productivity increase while we barely maintain

Accelerated by the law into that prophecy called "being at one with risk"

"In architecture," the economist says, "no one would ever put efficiency before safety," just in the market place

Where our myth of being first takes precedent they decree value and the whole realm of nature quakes

Sovereignty's indwelling flames are invisible hands

Here come the new machines while productivity gains they put down the wage earner

What remains is the gleam of planned obsolescence

The archival designs of the whole world left behind by fate

The world made relatable through a few names.

—for Claire Pentecost

‡

"An exercise is the heart"

An exercise is the heart
Before there was any attachment
To the garbage that was man
That died, that was, again

"I heart," do you remember when
It was cool to say "I heart"?
Words like hearts drift down
The pages, animated GIFs
They even remember recent
Conflicts US taxes pay for

What the poets forget
Too *avant-garde* or not *avant-garde* enough?
Hard to decide
The way class warfare and genocide
Stick to the ribs

Project your own anthems without them
Lodge your skin your soul in public space
Anathema to this war against the dead
War against animal potential inside us
Fertility to change existence

A (glory) hole if I am blind to no suffering
Writes these lines someday someone will know what

They mean contemporary to them but
Maybe not now smear the world on your body
No one owns your body I will be present to
You if you promise to be present to me
When we are dead what it matters what
We have loved

Intended to be silly disobedience qua innocents
Fuck the world up in reverse reverse the
Smack down in backward motions descend
To rise like a film I want to believe

In the fire crowning our heads
Unspeakably real like fearless speech
Proceed through the misshapen
Sloughing-off eternity
Social antagonism
Like ghosts do

They project space
They perfect a public
Speech in private
With their private parts
Of speech

Phonemes democratize
The mouth one is really
Here because we are all

Here in hell, together
"Why can't we have a
100% survival rate?," Robert asks,
The patient being
Universal condition of
An embodied commons

Words form objective existence of love
The order they're in
Mediating
Love for the
Body/world

Garbage even—

Write our names profane
Instruments so the world
Will be better

Crown our tongues with flame

The point of poems is recognition
Recognition of death so there is no more fear

The terrible things the world has done to us vanish

The terrible things we have done
To the world inspire us to act.

—after CA Conrad's *A Beautiful Marsupial Afternoon*

‡

The Hegemon Say

Mouth to hand
What remains from *nostos*
Surfeit like surfaces
Flash exilic

Hand in mouth
Mothers in excess
Recessed like
This shore just moved

Tongue in hand
Those sayings we say
To sooth not smooth
Tautology over

In flame these sayings
What they say
Have struck
Mark of the mouth

Adrift in flame
Who are we
Called into being
By being alone

Who moves us mother
Father where have
You gone
To be like all fathers

Where have you gone
The sun used to rise
In your spirit
Now just a notion

Puns on disuse
Can't see the words
For their truth
Goes up in flames

Like this is the open
We're discovered in
An open mouth
Whose contents are flame

Open quotation marks
Like wings in air
Never taking flight
They just take and take

Singing disuse
What won't we estrange
So abstract these words
They must be singular

No God ever suffered
Like you suffer
Entered into a history
Of stutters

Of mispronounced names
Shit like the hegemon say
When it's riled
To take names

Write unusefully
A sometimes lyrically
Impossible burden
Nations iterate

Like films we repeat
To collaborate with the present
Because one is not here
To say it

Too much transcendent
Talk too much flame
Is not presence
You are burning me forever

Father you are burning
I just woke up
History exceeds every
Nightmare I've ever had

Of you I am not you
But you make us you
Pronouns shift and compound
This is different than removing them

Into allegory the community
Of those who had to write
Engendered by gerunds
Endangered by gestus.

—after Theresa Hak Kyung Cha

‡

Debt (II)

Debtors take back the park
Against this "communism of the rich"
Take back the square for hoods
We are every one inside

The park we remark upon spring
Mourning not a matter of speech
For when we are all public
No speaking will be saved

We spring there is a debt
There is another
What we have mourned the loss of
The loss of those chains

All there is to lose
Transported by bodies in space
Virtual credits we will pay
Back in peace times

No time for bullion leveraging
Rights to this actual dance
Transported by proximity
The sun does not come out

But it feels like spring anyway
I can only imagine
What art will do
On the other side of occupation

Right now the art of going to jail
The art of being bailed-out
The art of legal fees
"Our rap sheets, ourselves" (Buuck)

"What are you doing in there?"
"What are you doing out there?"
(Emerson & Thoreau)
Dialectics of jail time and being sprung

The poetics of white cuffs
Slowly the truth comes out and it hurts
Who hears the sleeping leaves at night?
What art would be without its value

In the marketplace?
Who we will owe when this is over?
What you will miss is longing to end
The utopian longing in remote controlled boats

On the pond in Central Park
Brought suddenly to a focus
By being in public unquieted
What Olmstead dreamt is spreading

Spread the debt around
Here is a credit
You can use anywhere
A debt owed to the season

Paid in future generations
Who the people are in the future
Do they still breathe air like us
Luxuriate in walking dogs pond-side

As in a Schuyler hymn?
What the opposite of *momento mori* is
Remember to live
Virtuosity of budding and going to jail

Who will be left to jail us
If we are all in jail
Though it is no wish of mine
Winter lingers in the mind

Other seasons more pastoral
Than this one can be
Don't forget to put ordinary things in your poems
Things that should most of all remind us

What we owe
Written in blood like the things we make
Like a ledger of bad faith
Think of the things you take

For granted then take
Some of them away
Enabling yourself through this process
Try to write a poem

That will actualize those powers
You didn't know you had
Like a credit
Like a secret debt.

—for David Buuck, after reading David Graeber's *Debt*

‡

All We're Demanding Is the World

My friend Robert says that the only thing he won't allow them to take away from him is his ability to give everything away

Sitting in Dana's kitchen in Cincinnati

Transected by urgencies we will only seem to be present to in the live stream of police unreadied

When what we want and what we're demanding is nothing less than the world

Fugue of world-ending powers no apocalypto Mayan calendar bullshit

Whose 90s will come back with all the force of Hamlet's ghost

Reminds me I am a child of that future past

Like Brian repeats those lines about Hong Kong banking in his book *False Intimacy*

Origins come into focus—traumatic scenes of our appearance

We are the symptoms of endless commons never granted, never upheld

Blocked forms of intimacy dreaming of John of Runnymede forced to sign the Magna Carta by his lords

Whatever antinomies condition the distribution of the sensible a poetics dreams this

I/thou becomes the Facebook thread the Twitter feed just above some threshold of what we could feel positing the prosodic organs required to sense “x”

The people were always an emanation of lost time/displaced space/ placeless places

The lyricism of bodies no longer physically present to us

Like the People’s Microphone not only amplifies but inscribes, I began to imagine a generation founded on direct political processes

Someone suddenly taking agenda items in the ruins of consumer culture, calling out points of procedure in a mall or supermarket

This community that isn’t one—singular-multiple—makes possible a horizon where the people will recognize themselves

Where we will take back everything that already belonged to us.

‡

Time Stamps

There's a totally different way to do this and we know it

A totally different way to pay for labor, to put money in a bank, to think about banks and money and effort

Bling and spirit and bling and spirit and bling and spirit and bling and spirit

Eléna is right when she says more people should take responsibility for their own minds, totally aware of how much we've internalized our subjugation

To feel the heft of something that makes sense and then have it effervesce

Like they took the books away, the books become even more beautiful with their withdrawal

Likewise, the people become more beautiful, the idea of the people, with every eviction

Those who were living in the park from day one—sacral

Drifting into enunciations that are not formations

Parsing the difference between police forces—New York's is an army, Oakland's a band of thugs

What amount of love it will take to make things right?

The young become a poem of force anticipating an era that was not
defined by objective violence

Not even demanding paradise, just that rights be enforced, the
withdrawal of resources be rectified

Double consciousness of having a job, double vision of the Live Stream

Where we are in time, and where we are in space, and where we are
in the media

A delay in glass because two windows were open in Safari makes me
wish I was recording this

When we think we wish we were recording this what posterity could
we possibly have in mind?

Are those people we are imagining in the future like us, not entirely
without hope?

There is a mood of end times and there is a mood of Kafka but these
are not the moods I'm in

Anything could happen

More than anything I want the conditions that make it possible for
you to read this poem to wither

It is like memoir, what we are doing, it is like shout-outs into the future anterior

Some void or vacuum we will have produced ourselves in beyond what cris calls "the nightmare of we"

This is the us I want to produce, finally

The youth who slept in the park from day one now walks dogs to make some income

All friendship, as Dana recognizes, is an effort of forthcoming

Not everything we "didn't talk about," but the conditions we created for speaking with each other again in the future

Nursing those greetings contra the violence that would vanquish duration, human duration at least

My sense of time is different now

As though some world shimmered just beyond our efforts to see it

The new organs of perception we would need to cultivate in order to understand it

Wondering why we have inboxes anymore

Wondering if these buildings will be here in a year

I don't want the world to vanish, or be destroyed, just to be totally altered

Mate with the ones you want to become, like Bhanu says

The time of singing is over because they are amassing armies to stop the world from occurring.

‡

Acknowledgments

I owe an immense debt of gratitude to Michael Cross for encouraging the publication of this book since 2012 and for his ever-excellent design work. I also owe a debt of thanks to Harris Johnson for producing and allowing Compline permission to reproduce his intriguing phonemic drawings.

The poems collected here have appeared in numerous journals and magazines, and as chapbooks. Thanks and praise are due to Joel Allegretti, for publishing parts of "True Black (II)" in *Rabbit Ears: TV Poems*; to Andrea Rexilius, for soliciting "Area" for *Bombay Gin*; to Cassandra Troyan, for publishing parts of "True Black (II)" in *Fanzine*; to Adam Fitzgerald, for publishing "Blood Moon" in the second issue of *Maggy*; to Brett Price, for publishing "The Commons" in the inaugural publication of American Books, *Solicitations*; to Judah Rubin, for publishing "'An exercise is the heart,'" "Debt (II)," and "Where it proceeds to the rupture" in his *The Death and Life of Great American Cities*; to Anselm Berrigan, for publishing "All I Wanted Was to Be in a Band" in *The Brooklyn Rail*; to Luke McMullan and Sophie Seita, who published a version of "Blood Moon" in their journal *1**; to Ana Božičević and Amy King, for publishing "Since Zuccotti" in their magazine, *Esque*; to Nathan Austin, for publishing "Time Stamps" during his stint as visiting editor of *Joyland Poetry*; to Aryanil Mukherjee and Pat Clifford, who published significant portions of the first part of this book online via their *MUD Project*; to Mónica de la Torre, who published "The New Us" in *BOMB*; to Dan Thomas-Glass, for publishing "The Leak" in *With + Stand*; to Maw

Shein Win, who put Fred Tomaselli and myself in touch, prompting me to compose "An Archive of Eyes" for *See | Saw*; to *The Offending Adam*, for publishing parts of "True Black (I)"; to Maj Hasager, for her use and publication of the poem beginning with the line "Spilled in the language's veins" for her project, *Making Invisible*; and to Michael Cross, for his design and publication of "The Hegemon Say" as a chapbook with Compline.

For those who have invited me to their reading series and event spaces to read these poems, thank you!

Many of the individuals named in this book have contributed to a companion book—a book of "metadiscourse"—based upon this one. I would like to thank them for taking the time to read and provide responses to *Withdrawn* when it was in manuscript, which are included in *Shifter* 23, *Withdrawn: a Discourse.*

To all those who participated in the Occupy movement, many of these poems are marked by and indeed still move through that event.

I dedicate this book to my friends, family, students, and comrades who consistently bring me back from my periodic withdrawals.

COMPLIN

COHMPLIIY

COMPLINE.

COMPLIYNE

COMPLAIYN

COHMPLINE